COURSE DESIGN FOR COLLEGE TEACHERS

COURSE DESIGN FOR COLLEGE TEACHERS

LARRY LOVELL-TROY, PhD
Department of Behavioral Sciences
Millikin University

PAUL EICKMANN, PhD
Vice President for Academic Affairs
Cleveland Institute of Art

EDUCATIONAL TECHNOLOGY PUBLICATIONS
ENGLEWOOD CLIFFS, NEW JERSEY 07632

Library of Congress Cataloging-in-Publication Data

Lovell-Troy, Lawrence Allen.
　　Course design for college teachers / Larry Lovell-Troy, Paul
Eickmann.
　　　　p.　cm.
　　Includes bibliographical references (p.　) and index.
　　ISBN 0-87778-239-3
　　1. College teaching--United States.　I. Eickmann, Paul.
II. Title.
LB2331.L67　1992
378.1'25'0973--dc20　　　　　　　　　　　　　　　　91-31295
　　　　　　　　　　　　　　　　　　　　　　　　　　　　CIP

Printed in the United States of America.

Library of Congress Catalog Card Number:
91-31295.

International Standard Book Number:
0-87778-239-3.

First Printing:　January 1992.

TABLE OF CONTENTS

vi

PREFACE

This book began with the dream of one man, Paul Eickmann. It evolved from more than a decade of experience presenting the ideas in workshop form to several hundred college teachers, and was finally brought to fruition by the collaboration of Eickmann and Larry Lovell-Troy. The story is worth repeating, since it contributes to an understanding of the basic themes of the book, i.e., it is important to dream, to let ideas mature and develop over time, and to involve colleagues in developing courses.

In the mid-1970s, Paul Eickmann was working as a course developer at Syracuse University's Center for Instructional Development with Bob Diamond. In those same years, the Lilly Foundation provided a broadly-defined grant for instructional, institutional, and professional faculty development to the twelve liberal arts colleges of the Great Lakes Colleges Association. At the termination of the Lilly grant in 1977, the GLCA distilled the best of what they had learned from two experimental summer conferences by creating a week-long summer workshop to focus exclusively on teaching. Paul was brought in as a consultant to the workshop, with particular focus on course design. He taught the GLCA staff members and former Lilly Fellows the structure and perspective of the Syracuse model of course design, adapting it to the styles of small college faculty members. Within a few years, the GLCA Workshop on Course Design and Teaching became well-established with a regular staff that included Paul Eickmann, Peter Frederick, Julie Jeffrey, Oliver Loud, the late Nan Nowick, and Stephen Scholl.

Larry Lovell-Troy joined the workshop as a participant in 1984. He had come to work on his own teaching at Millikin University and to learn the craft of faculty development from the staff. Millikin had just appointed him Consultant on Teaching and Learning, a quarter-time position modeled after a similar one at Earlham College, which itself was an outcome from the 1974 Lilly grant. In 1986, Larry joined the staff of the Workshop on Course Design and Teaching, as intern to Paul. The intent was to expand the responsibility within the workshop for course design. This highly successful workshop is still continuing, and further information about it is available from the GLCA.

Over the years, the dual goals of the GLCA Workshop (course design and teaching) became more integrated based on the feedback of the participants and the experience of the staff, now administered by Jeanine Elliott and including Kit Price and Dave Finster in addition to Peter, Julie, Ollie, Larry, and Paul. That integration involved adaptations of the model of course design, which Bob Diamond and the Syracuse University Center have used so successfully in the university context. These adaptations for college teachers at liberal arts colleges pushed the focus of course design away from a reliance on instructional development staff and technique and toward a more holistic view of course design, teaching skills, and strategies.

During these years, Paul and Larry spoke often about Paul's dream to develop the course design ideas into a workbook to enable faculty on all college campuses to benefit from both the adapted Syracuse model and the related workshop ideas on teaching. As Vice-President for Student Affairs at Syracuse, Paul lacked the time to devote to such a project. Larry's sabbatical in 1988 provided the time to begin to adapt the ideas and fashion them into their present form. He is the author of this book, but the original dream, ideas, and vision came from Paul.

Clearly, however, the authors are both indebted to the staff of the GLCA workshop who helped clarify and implement many of the ideas found in this book, and to the hundreds of workshop participants who gave them feedback and struggled with the ideas in their own processes of course development and teaching improvement. The GLCA staff provided feedback on earlier drafts of this workbook, as did Bob Diamond, Mary Deane Sorcinelli, and Maryellen Weimer. Their time and wisdom are appreciated, even if all their suggestions were not heeded. Larry would like to thank Laura Birch and Larry Songer at Millikin University's Mueller Computer Center for their help in rescuing him from the intricacies of Word Perfect. Finally, both Paul and

Larry also acknowledge the patience and help of Lawrence Lipsitz from Educational Technology Publications, who extended deadlines and provided encouragement as the ideas matured and developed over two and a half years. We could not have completed this book without the help of all these people.

Larry Lovell-Troy
Paul Eickmann
May 1991

COURSE DESIGN FOR COLLEGE TEACHERS

INTRODUCTION

Designing a course is probably one of the most misunderstood aspects of college teaching. Most frequently, for example, we are told to teach Introduction to Sociology, Organic Chemistry, Music Theory, or some other course. In fact, we may have been hired by our university to teach that particular course, and we are well-prepared to teach it. We may have taken such a course in our own undergraduate education, studied its content in depth during graduate school, and even conducted research or published in the field.

Teaching this course should be a breeze. Typically, we choose a few textbooks, from among the several dozen sent us by publishers, peruse them, and select the one that seems to fit best with how we conceive the field. Chapter 1 becomes Week 1, and we are off and running!

Nevertheless, problems may surface. Midway through the semester we may begin to get bored and sense that students feel the same way. We may tell ourselves we are "going over the field," but a malaise creeps into our teaching. The book is acceptable; our lectures, discussions, and other instructional strategies all seem appropriate; still, something is not right. Depending upon the sophistication of faculty and instructional development on our campus, we may even seek help, but don't really know what to ask. So we probably muddle through and finish the course, perhaps vowing to make it better next time.

The problem is we don't really know how to make it better! We have been teaching a course designed by others, following accepted conventional wisdom in our discipline, without considering *what we* want to teach, *how we* want to teach it, *whom we* are teaching, and *why* it should be taught. The answer to our problem lies in a more systematic approach to course design.

There are several approaches to course design in the literature. *Designing the Learning Plan: A Review of Research and Theory Related to College Curricula* by Stark and Lowther is a comprehensive review of the literature on the subject. Most approaches include the same steps, and involve describing the learners, preparing instructional objectives, planning learning activities, and deciding on teaching strategies. The main difference among these various approaches is the order in which these steps are executed.

The authors of the present book take the position that the order in which these activities are accomplished does not matter, as long as they are accomplished. What is more important, and what sets this book apart from other approaches to course design, is that we believe it is important to gather as much information as possible about your course, your students, and your sources, as well as to question as many of your initial conceptions about the course as possible, *before arriving at those common design steps.*

A book with an approach similar to ours is *Designing and Improving Courses and Curricula in Higher Education* by Robert M. Diamond. The two works stem from the same perspective on course design, especially since Paul Eickmann worked with Diamond for many years. The two books differ, however, in conception and intended audience.

The Diamond book is a major addition to the theoretical literature on course design. It describes in a sensible way the process of curriculum design as developed and practiced at Syracuse University, one of the leading institutions in the world in this field. The examples shown in the Diamond book are a striking testimony to what can be accomplished and how courses and programs can be developed with the assistance of a well-organized, supportive, and fully-staffed instructional development office. Although some readers of the Diamond book may be individual faculty members, its main audience is college or university adminis- trators and staff members of instructional or faculty develop- ment offices. The book also addresses curriculum design involving an entire department, school, or college. It is unlikely that an individual faculty member will pick up the book and use it to design his or her own course.

We conceive of our book as a companion to the Diamond volume, i.e., a workbook to which college faculty may refer *by themselves and/or with one or two colleagues* in the process of designing their own courses. Interested readers would benefit immensely from reading Diamond's book and studying its diagrams, evaluation instruments, and examples. Our conception in writing this book, however, is that most college teachers do not have access to a fully-staffed, instructional development office. Also, they are busy enough teaching, keeping up in their own fields, serving on committees, doing research or writing, and maintaining their families to have the time to master the literature of instructional design on their own. Nevertheless, there should be something available for these college teachers to help them in the design of their courses. That is the gap which the present book fills.

OVERVIEW OF
THE PROCESS

The objective of this book is to take you through a process which will result in a course *you* design. Contrary to many other books on course design, though, this book will require your active involvement. We will ask you to think, write, question, seek out answers or information, and constantly to consider and reconsider aspects of your course. To benefit from our suggestions, you will have to participate in the process, so we have designed the book with perforated pages and worksheets. This active involvement is as it should be, because only you can design your course. We have provided you with a process or a framework that you can use, but the creative energy and the commitment must come from you.

An organizing assumption for the course design process described in this book is that you are starting from ground zero and designing a totally new course. Nevertheless, different readers will use this book at different stages of course design for different courses. It may be that you have already taught the course, perhaps a number of times, and are looking for ways to improve it. Or you may have a perfectly acceptable course, and are simply skimming this

7

book for one or two small changes or additions to the course. Another possibility might be that you wish to change a major section of a course, while leaving the remainder intact. Whatever your situation, this book will help you develop a course which will be richer, more diverse, more attuned to student needs, more accountable to various constituencies in the classroom or the community, and more satisfying to teach than others you have taught before.

A further organizing assumption of the course design process outlined in this book is that it is not a process that can be accomplished alone, or too quickly. We ask you to find one or two colleagues from different disciplines who will volunteer to go through the process with you, criticizing your course design, and offering insights. By placing themselves in the role of the student, they can question assumptions you make and help you to clarify complex points. Ideally, each of you should be planning a course at the same time; your motivation to help each other will be increased as you realize the help you are receiving. Further, this process cannot be accomplished in the week before the course starts. The steps we will take you through require time, with the ideas developing and enriching themselves as they mature and build on each other. Therefore, you should expect that you and your colleagues might take a semester or a summer to plan your courses.

The process starts with **GATHERING** information. As we indicated in the Introduction, the activity of gathering as much information as possible about your course and the students *before* you begin to plan the course is a very important one. The first several steps of the course design process are intended to help you *expand* your initial conception of your course, beyond that conventionally considered in your discipline. This is an important beginning, because it offers you the greatest chance of designing the best course you can. The process starts with *gathering* information designed to address the question of whether or not the course should be taught in the first place. The more information you can gather, the richer your course will be. You will produce a course description from this **GATHERING** process which should include a review of the content of the course from as many points of view as possible (the standards of the discipline, professionals in the field, students, practitioners, administrators, potential employers).

The **GATHERING** process continues with a consideration of who the students are, because courses should not be designed without early reflection about those to whom the course is directed. We will ask you some questions about your students and offer you some ideas about how you can think about your students' level of development and readiness for your course.

This step continues with a focus on the content of the course. You are asked to list as many concepts, ideas, practices, and activities as you can imagine that could be relevant to your course. We also ask you to compile as many resources as possible to be used in the learning and teaching of the course. We further ask you to consider alternate or possibly innovative sources of learning for you and your students.

Throughout this process we will have you seek out your colleagues from different disciplines to *question* everything you initially conceive: your description of your course and your students, as well as the proposed content and learning resources. The better the questions and challenges, the more developed your course will be. These questioning sessions should then send you back to the design process as you consider the critiques and suggestions of your colleagues.

Taken together, **GATHERING** is extremely important in the development of your course. If the course is entirely new for you, it is important to consider the course carefully and defend it against all possible criticisms. Such early consideration clarifies the course in your own mind and helps you decide whether the course should actually be taught and in what form. If you have taught the course before, such challenging and forced re-conceptualizations are also important since they provide the opportunity to expand previous course designs and enrich what has become standard or stale. The more information you can gather, the more critiques, challenges, and trials you can put the course through in the initial design of it, the better the course will be when you finally teach it.

The second step in the course design process is the actual **PLANNING** of the course. As we did in the **GATHERING** stage, we will continue to push you to plan the best course you can. We start this stage by asking you to expand the content list you developed by *dreaming*. This strategy is designed to help you improve your course by breaking through self-imposed barriers and thinking about enriching possibilities.

Through an innovative set of concepts, we will next help you *analyze and organize* the results of your dreaming by assisting you to set some priorities and to order the major points. The result will be an organized and innovative course that will be more interesting to teach and better organized and involving for the students.

The final stage of the course design process is IMPLEMENTING your newly-designed course. At this point you *elaborate* each unit of the course. This step is similar to many others found in the traditional course design literature. We will ask you to consider the learners again, prepare instructional objectives, evaluate or design instructional resources, and consider teaching strategies. This latter process takes us into the burgeoning field of instructional development which has been promoting the use of active learning methods of teaching.

TEACHING the course is actually one more step in the process of course design, because no course is perfect; no course should remain static from semester to semester. Teaching the course also helps you in EVALUATING your own course. More formal evaluation from students, both formative and summative, is finally solicited to provide you with the important feedback that only the learners in a course can provide. Ideally, you would then repeat the whole process prior to teaching the course again.

Although we have just presented the process in a linear fashion, working through the process is distinctly non-linear. Several times we will suggest you return to earlier stages; at other times, we will urge you on even though you have not completed the previous step. This is as it should be because the development process is a creative one. New awarenesses and ideas will necessarily change or expand earlier results.

Serendipitous discoveries while dreaming or elaborating may require changes in the information and ideas you gathered earlier. Feedback you will get from colleagues and students will result in revisions of the course before you actually teach it, as well as in subsequent semesters.

In sum, this book takes you through a process that will help you to create a course based upon your perceptions of the needs of the students, college, university, and community. Your particular areas of expertise will form the basis of the course, but other areas will be easily and usefully added to enrich it. This process, however, is different from that traditionally followed. It requires commitment and an active involvement with the design of your course. We strongly believe you will be well-rewarded for your time and effort with a course that is distinctly unique to you!

GATHERING

♦ **Describe Your Course**

♦ **Describe the Learners**

♦ **Prepare a Content List**

♦ **Prepare a Resources List**

GATHERING

GATHERING is an extremely important part of the course design process. It is the step left out or glossed over too frequently, resulting in poorly conceptualized courses which become difficult and unexciting to teach. The primary purpose of GATHERING is to collect as much information about your course as possible, resulting in a broader conception of it. Four aspects of the course need to be considered in detail at this point: a course description, a description of the learners or students, a content list, and a list of sources for the content of the course. In this first stage, it is necessary for you to gather as much information as possible about the students and the course you are designing.

As you proceed, keep your mind open to expanding your view of what is possible in the course. Most likely, this course has been taught many times before, by many others in your field. An established, conventional wisdom has developed about the content of the course and how it should be taught. The **GATHERING** stage is designed to help you challenge that conventional wisdom. Only by confronting your initial ideas and challenging them can you arrive at a course that is yours, and that is better, because it draws on your strengths, your knowledge, and the opportunities available to you at your school.

Therefore, postpone the tendency to sit down with a calendar and map out Mondays, Wednesdays, and Fridays. Resist taking out your old graduate school notes and applying them to your own students. Let the **GATHERING** stage of course design develop at its own pace. This approach will mature and enrich your course, as you let it proceed.

As we noted in the Overview, the process of course design can be helped immeasurably if you conduct it with a colleague. Before proceeding, therefore, it would be wise for you to choose a colleague or two to work with you. Ideally, these people should be ones with whom you can talk freely, and can trust to be honest, fair, encouraging, interested, critical, and open. It is also important that they be from disciplines different from your own, because our disciplinary boundaries create blinders making it difficult to conceive of our courses in new ways. Those who have shared our training also share our conceptions of what the course is "supposed" to look like. Conversely, when you are pushed to develop your course with an interested, knowledgeable lay-person, new insights appear.

Periodically, throughout this book, we will suggest that you consult with your colleagues to obtain feedback and criticism. Although the idea of these consultations may sound frightening at first, those feedback sessions will become enjoyable and extremely enlightening. Indeed, you may wonder how you ever accomplished similar projects without them.

A. Describe Your Course

The purpose of this step in the process is to develop a clear conception of the course you will teach, and to receive feedback from your colleagues. When you have completed it, you will have a more comprehensive understanding of the course from a variety of perspectives, and it should be richer and more interesting to you than you originally thought.

Let's engage in a fantasy or role play. Instead of just gathering information about your course, pretend you are proposing it to be taught at your college for the first time. What would you say? How would you defend it against critics? Should your course be taught? Who says so? Would you be open to changing it to accommodate reasonable objections? Do the following exercise.

Write a brief statement describing and criticizing your course. Include in your description as much information as you believe necessary to allow a colleague from a different discipline to understand the purpose and intent of the course. In your description, you might want to consider the following points:

* Describe the course briefly.
* How does it contribute to the curriculum of the department, school or college, university?
* What level of commitment exists, on the part of the students, yourself, the department, the institution?
* Should the course be taught? Why?
* Describe the positive aspects of working on and/or teaching this course.
* Describe the potential complications associated with developing and/or teaching this course.

Do this exercise on the worksheet.

_____   _____

      Course Name   Date

Course Description

_____

_____

_____

_____

_____

_____

_____

_____

_____

_____

_____

_____

_____

_____

_____

_____

_____

_____

_____

_____

_____

_____

_____

_____

_____

_____

_____

_____

_____

_____

_____

_____

_____

Once you have written this course description, show it to your colleagues, and defend it. The colleagues should not role-play being a student; rather, have them simply be interested potential learners. They could regard themselves as colleagues contemplating enrolling in the course during a sabbatical. They should challenge as many assumptions and assertions as possible. Does this sound like an interesting course? What might make it more interesting? Most often this questioning-and-suggesting session will present you with ideas you hadn't considered before that will enrich your course and make it more exciting.

This is a very important step in the process of preparing to teach a course, because it helps you begin to escape the constraints that your discipline places on you. It is the first step in truly making the course yours.

Following this session with your colleagues, revise your course description taking into account the critiques and suggestions offered to you. Remember, though, it is not mandatory that you *accept* all suggestions and criticisms; the course is still yours. Simply consider them since they have the potential to improve your course.

B. Describe the Learners

In gathering information about your course, more specific attention should be given to the students than is customary at this point. Courses should be designed to teach particular people. In effect, it is important to keep in mind that you are not teaching a course; you are enabling students to learn. The more you know about the learners, the better you will be able to design a course which will address them at their level and then help them get where you want them to be at the end of the course.

Therefore, at this point, write a description of the students. You need to consider:

* Are these majors or non-majors?
* What year in school? (Freshmen, Seniors, Graduate Students, Community People, etc.)
* What do these students need from the course?
* What are their probable relevant skills, attitudes, knowledge, abilities, interests?
* What skills, attitudes, knowledge, abilities, appreciations do you want the students to have when they leave the course?

Do this exercise on the next worksheet.

_____   _____
    Course Name   Date

The Learners

_____

_____

_____

_____

_____

_____

_____

_____

_____

_____

_____

_____

A further important consideration about the students is their expected level of intellectual development. One of the more useful models on student intellectual development is that developed by William Perry. (See *Forms of Intellectual and Ethical Development in the College Years* if you are interested in reading more about this model.) Briefly, Perry argues that students develop through nine distinct developmental "positions," which can be usefully summarized as falling into three stages. Through the progress of this development young people change in their ability to comprehend the difference between information and knowledge, to understand the roles of teachers and students, and to make decisions within the complexities of social and personal life.

The first stage, called *dualism*, involves a "right-or-wrong" view of the world. Knowledge is a collection of facts to be memorized, and teachers are authority figures with all the answers. These students will probably be uncomfortable in courses with a great deal of discussion; what is important to them is to get the right answers, and those always come from the authority figure, the teacher.

At the second stage, referred to as *multiplicity,* uncertainty is acknowledged in some areas, but where facts are not known all opinions are seen as equally valid. Students can recognize the existence of a variety of opinions and viewpoints on an issue, but often do not have the ability to evaluate logically or ethically the veracity or consistency of the various positions. Students at this position are likely to throw their hands up at a class discussion or a debate, because they see such exercises as simply the expression of different, equally valid viewpoints. Like the dualists, they may get impatient, waiting for the teacher to provide the class with the right answers, or, on the other hand, they may question the statements from teachers since they are simply someone else's opinions.

Students at the third stage, known as *relativism,* can understand and appreciate that facts are often a function of context, and decisions need to be based on some supporting criteria like logic or consistency. Relativists come to see authorities as simply more experienced learners in a particular field. These students are more ready than those at earlier stages to develop the skills of rational discourse, of supporting positions with evidence, and of using logic to critique ideas and opinions. They will be more likely to learn from class discussion and debate, since it will provide them with opportunities to practice their skills and understandings.

A recent critique of Perry's work is found in *Women's Ways of Knowing* by Belenky, Clinchy, Goldberger, and Tarule. Based on the earlier work of Carol Gilligan, the argument here is that women go through somewhat different stages and have different ways of expressing themselves and understanding knowledge than originally found by Perry, who did much of his research on men at Harvard. This view asserts that women may start with a position called *received knowledge.* Like Perry's dualists, women in such a position count on authorities to supply them with right answers. Truth for these learners is external. A second mode of knowing is one they call *subjectivism.* This is the opposite of received knowledge in that truth is found internally, or based on feelings. The final developmental step is known as *procedural knowledge* in which the learner has systematic, deliberate procedures for developing new ideas or for testing the validity of ideas. (See "Issues of Gender in Teaching and Learning" by Clinchy for a brief discussion of these views and their implications for teaching.)

The Belenky *et al.* book concludes with specific teaching implications of their findings. Most important among these is that professors need to begin their course design with a consideration of what the student already knows. More specifically, we need to focus more on the knowledge that students bring to the classroom, support those students in the evolution of their own thinking, and create classroom situations that allow for discussion of ideas without an adversarial climate.

It is probably not important to know the exact stage at which your students fall, either in the Perry or the Belenky *et al.* model. Some research suggests that most entry-level freshmen are at Perry's stage of late dualism, and that many, if not most, seniors are only at the multiplicity stage. As you consider and describe your course, expect younger students to be more or less dualistic in their thinking, while older ones are probably more likely to be multiplicists. The best strategy seems to be to follow the Belenky *et al.* suggestions: meet the students at their general level and then, through supportive challenges, move them along in their development. When you are designing your course, diversity in the classroom should be respected by providing objectives and teaching strategies for different learners. Furthermore, we need to respect the viewpoints, perspectives, and knowledge of the students, *as they come into our classrooms.* We will return to this point later when we more specifically consider learning objectives and teaching strategies.

Consider at this point the specific relevance of this conception of students to your course. How do the ideas of Perry and Belenky *et al.* fit with your initial conceptualization of your course? More generally, what are the implications of the total description of the learners for your course, as you described it in the previous step? Does the course as you described it above still make sense? Are there implications for the coverage of specific content areas, either the addition of some or the skipping of others? Should you consider some elements of remediation? Are there other changes you need to make to fit the course better to the students?

Answer these questions on the next worksheet.

_____   _____

Course Name   Date

Implications of Perry and
Belenky *et al.* on
this course

_____

_____

_____

_____

_____

_____

_____

_____

_____

_____

_____

_____

_____

_____

_____

Discuss these ideas with your colleagues. What are their reactions? You might want to rewrite portions of your course description after you have considered these issues and consulted with your colleagues.

We feel a need to offer you some support at this stage of the process. The questions we have been suggesting that you consider can be difficult ones. You may have begun to resist the reconceptualizations we have recommended for a variety of reasons. Perhaps you are feeling the weight of your discipline on your back. For example, some exasperated faculty members have told us, "Nobody ever considered these things before in teaching Introduction to Chemistry!" (or Calculus, or Modern English Literature.) Others have complained at this point, "How am I to consider remediation when I don't have the time to teach what needs to be taught already?"

If you have been feeling these constraints, please bear with us. They are common concerns. It *may be* that no one felt the need to consider these questions previously. But no one has taught *your* particular students before either. It *may be* that you are already pressed for time in the coverage of your material. But again, bear with us! We will show you later how you can get more content into your course than you thought possible. What we are after is a *better* course than you would have taught if you hadn't gone through this process. Detailed consideration of the students at this point will help make your course a successful one, since the students will be more likely to learn the content you feel is important. Isn't that what you are after, in the final analysis?

C. Prepare a Content List

Now that you've described your course and the learners, and received feedback on these descriptions, it is time to consider the content of the course. What is it, exactly, that you want the students to learn? Notice that the question is not, "What do you want to teach in this course?" Students will learn many things from various sources. The next section will develop this point. For now, however, it is important to think about your course content from the students' perspective.

On the next worksheet, write a list of content that you want the students in your course to learn. Be as general or specific as you feel you have to be. Look through texts that may be traditionally used in this course, but do not be confined to them. Look through your other books and journals; consult others in your field; review your notes from your discussions with your colleagues. Make a list of all possible things that could be learned in the course. At this point do not worry if the list is too long or too short. We will help you expand it even further later on, as well as analyze and organize it. The important point is: If you do not put it down on paper, you will probably not teach it. If you do put it down, we will help you fit most of it in.

Course Name   Date

Content List

_____

_____

_____

_____

_____

_____

_____

_____

_____

_____

_____

_____

_____

Show this list to your colleagues. *Engage in a brainstorming session with them.* The ultimate goal of this session is a content list that is larger than you compiled by yourself. This step is important because it helps you enrich your course with content you have not previously considered. Graduate training often narrows us by establishing boundaries for traditional coverage of specific courses. This exercise will expand your course, by breaking down your disciplinary blinders. Use the next worksheet to expand the list you developed above.

Course Name   Date

Expanded Content List

D. Prepare a Resources List

What learning resources will you and the students use in teaching and learning the content you have just listed? This is an important question and one that needs to be asked at this point. One answer chosen by many college teachers, especially relatively inexperienced ones and those who are overworked or teaching a new course without adequate time for preparation, is to assign a textbook for the students to read, while finding lecture material in a different textbook.

This practice can certainly work, but it is not the ideal for systematic course design. Textbooks are written by people, and are the expression of the course as those people conceive it. They are also often written by committees, even when one name is listed as the author. Is your conception of the field exactly the same as that produced by a committee? Look at your course description and content list, especially after you revised them based on the critiques you solicited. Are all those issues covered in the textbooks? Are your students the same as those for whom the textbook was written?

A further consideration in these times of higher publication costs is that textbook publishers try to hit certain broad markets in the creation of their books. While many of these books are certainly good, they will be quite different from what you are beginning to conceive as you develop your *own* course. By definition, those books are meant to be average. Your course is not going to be average.

Therefore, the question posed above becomes a relevant one. *You* are the expert in this field on your campus, at the

very least for *your* students. What learning resources will
you rely on to prepare for this course? What learning
resources will you make available or assign to your students
from which they can learn?

As a first attempt to answer these questions, write a
learning resource list for your course on the next worksheet.
You may want to conceptualize this in two ways. First, what
are the resources to which you can refer in preparing the
lectures, discussions, assignments, etc.? Second, what are
resources the students may be assigned to read, see, consult,
or experience? In developing these lists, refer to your course
description, as it was revised after the critique by colleagues.
Consider these questions as you develop these lists:

*   Where can you and the students go?
*   What can you and the students see or hear?
*   What can you and the students read?
*   What can you and the students do?
*   To whom can you and the students talk?

The worksheet for this exercise is on the next page.
Read on, though, before starting this task. In doing this
exercise, most faculty first turn to established texts, journals,
library materials, and perhaps laboratory exercises to begin
these lists. That is certainly appropriate. All should be
covered; do not leave possible resources off the list. But also
try to make your lists more comprehensive than is normally
considered in your field. Do all the resources have to be
printed? Are there media sources or other resources at your

_____   _____

Course Name   Date

Learning Resources List

Resources for Me   Students' Resources

_____   _____

_____   _____

_____   _____

_____   _____

_____   _____

_____   _____

_____   _____

_____   _____

_____   _____

_____   _____

_____   _____

_____   _____

Resources for Me   Students' Resources

_____   _____

_____   _____

_____   _____

_____   _____

_____   _____

_____   _____

_____   _____

_____   _____

_____   _____

_____   _____

_____   _____

_____   _____

_____   _____

_____   _____

_____   _____

_____   _____

university that you can use? What about in your community? What about museums, government offices, businesses, sites of historical significance, eminent people, locations in the community or on your campus where they do the kind of thing you are teaching, or some variant of it? Include these kinds of resources on your list. This suggestion may sound blasphemous to some, ridiculous to others, while it may be eye-opening and intriguing to still others. The reaction may vary according to discipline. Courses in some disciplines, such as sociology or history, may be amenable to such diverse resources. Admittedly, teachers in other fields, such as calculus or philosophy, may have a more difficult time. Nevertheless, the challenge is to try to expand your resource lists beyond those normally found in courses in your discipline. We have yet to find *any* course that could not be expanded and made more diverse by adding innovative sources of content. Invariably, the result of this process is a richer, more interesting and diverse course that has the potential to excite your students and help them to learn and enjoy your subject matter.

Remember your students. They are not like you. Generally, they are younger, less mature, and most importantly, they are less trained in learning the way you learn. For example, they may be less able to learn from reading difficult texts when they lack the background or ability. This does not mean, however, that you must give them fluff. It does mean that you must provide them with materials that will motivate them and prepare them to handle the more sophisticated materials. Do the exercise now.

After you have developed two lists, one for preparation and one for student assignments, combine the two.

Now have your colleagues critique your resources list. Engage your colleagues in another brainstorming session with the ultimate goal now being a resources list that is larger than you could have compiled by yourself. This step is as important here as it was for your course description and your content list. More than likely, you are still thinking too narrowly in terms of your own discipline and training. An interested layperson may come up with some very exciting and innovative learning possibilities, again because he or she does not share your blinders.

All suggestions, obviously, do not have to be heeded; you are still the final judge for your course. Nevertheless, give the suggestions of your colleagues an open consideration. They have the potential to broaden your perception of what students might be interested in, and all suggestions have the potential to enrich and broaden your course.

Then revise your content list and perhaps your course description to accommodate the suggestions provided by colleagues. It may be that suggestions of resources open up new ideas for actual content that you had not originally considered. Similarly, revisions in the course description may have implications for resources. Do not be afraid to consider all you have done so far as tentative and subject to change. Go back and forth revising course descriptions, content list, and resources list as they impact on each other.

Search out these resources now. Peruse the readings, review the exercises, visit the places, and talk to the people on your list. Keep your course description, profile of the students, and content list in mind. Do these resources fit with these descriptions and lists? If not, what needs to be changed? Could the course concept or content be broadened? Are the resources appropriate to the students' goals and levels of ability? Let these experiences begin to expand your conception of your course. Change your course description again to fit with new conceptions you may have just developed. Add to your content list and your resources list as you discover new sources of learning for you and your students.

Once you have revised the resources list you have completed the **GATHERING** stage of designing your course. You should now have a richer, more diverse conception of the course than you had before you went through this stage. You should have a better idea of who the students are and what their likely abilities and goals are, and how that may affect your course. And you should have a broader list of content and possible resources than you originally conceived. You are now ready to proceed with the planning of the course, but do not be afraid to return to the materials you developed to revise them still further as you proceed. Remember, nothing is final until you actually teach the course, and it may be changed the next time you teach it!

```
┌─────────────────────────────────────────┐
│                                         │
│           PLANNING                      │
│                                         │
│    ◆    Create a Dream List             │
│                                         │
│    ◆    Analyze Your Dream List         │
│                                         │
│    ◆    Diagram Your Course             │
│                                         │
│    ◆    Work Out the Timing             │
│                                         │
└─────────────────────────────────────────┘
```

PLANNING

You have now finished the important first steps in gathering information about your course. You've described and defended your course against criticism from colleagues, and presumably received valuable comments and suggestions in the process. These suggestions may have led you to revise your course description. The students as learners are now salient to you, and you have considered them in your conception of your course. You've also considered the course content, listed the learning resources, and received suggestions from colleagues which may have expanded your ideas for content, and perhaps provided ideas for the course itself.

Now it is time to begin the **PLANNING** process. This process begins with an ideal image of the course, and moves toward a more realistic one, which will include more of the ideal than you previously imagined. Your goal here is to develop as expansive and personal an image of your course as possible: expansive, because the more developed this image is, the better your course will ultimately be; personal, because you are the one teaching this course. The course should reflect your interests, skills, and you, not just the dictates of your discipline.

A. Create a Dream List

The first step in the **PLANNING** process is to develop a comprehensive, ideal picture of the course. You have begun this process already by writing a content list in the previous stage. We want you now, however, to expand it even further, by creating a *dream list.* We call this a *dream list* because we want you to imagine the best course you could teach on this topic and include everything you could possibly dream could be put into it.

Write Dream List I on the next worksheet, based on the following suggestions. Look again at your content and learning resource lists. Review the actual sources of content you listed and accumulate as many **additional content areas or topics** as possible which would be appropriate for this course. Consider also your goals or objectives for the course

<u>   </u>   <u>   </u>

Course Name   Date

Dream List I

_____

_____

_____

_____

_____

_____

_____

_____

_____

_____

_____

_____

_____

as outlined in your course description. Do they suggest content areas not found in the standard treatments of your subject? Think also about the skills, attitudes, or values you would like the students to acquire from your course. Add content areas that respond to these ideals. *In total, double the length of your content list by transforming it into a dream list.*

Fight the temptation to reject anything out of hand. Put down all ideas that come to you, no matter how outlandish; you can always throw out inappropriate items later. In the spirit of brainstorming, however, bad ideas often lead to good ones, so let the ideas flow and write them all down. We believe that this dreaming and expanding of content and of your conception of the course are some of the most important steps in course design. This is where the course you will teach distinguishes itself from the standard course offered by most others in your discipline.

We now want to help you expand your dream list even further. Let's engage in a fantasy or role play again, this time to write Dream List II, which is an extension of Dream List I.

Imagine now that the semester in which you taught the course has ended. The papers and exams have been graded. The course grades have been turned in to the registrar and you are ready for a well-deserved break. You are gathered informally with the students from the class at the local watering hole, student center, a party in your own home, or elsewhere. After a short time of party chatter, you get up your nerve and ask the students what they thought of the course. To your delight, they begin to tell you they loved it! One student says, "This was the best course I ever took because ..."

Finish the sentence. Finish the sentences of all the students in the class. Write as many completions of the sentence as you can imagine on the next worksheet.

Try not to let too much reality interfere with your dreaming. Add to your Dream List, by creating Dream List II, as you write down anything you can imagine your students would say. Let yourself dream! If the structure of the room you usually teach in constrains you, imagine teaching in a dream room. If the time constraint of one semester limits your dreaming, imagine no time limits. If the quality of the students you normally teach frustrates you, imagine the best students. If a budget restricts you, imagine all the money and resources you need.

Work on Dream List II before going on.

_____   _____

Course Name   Date

Dream List II

_____

_____

_____

_____

_____

_____

_____

_____

_____

_____

_____

_____

_____

Now write Dream List III on the next worksheet, **DOUBLING** *the length of the list, by thinking about the following variations from the students:*

"This was the best course I ever *took* because:

*   now I KNOW ..."
*   now I THINK ..."
*   now I FEEL ..."
*   now I CAN DO ..."
*   now I AM BECOMING ..."

Work on these variations before going on. Pay particular attention to what you imagine the students would tell you they *know* at this after-course session. This list should include as detailed a description as possible of all topics that students would know if you taught your *ideal course*. It is also important to pay attention to the more emotional or affective answers that you would like the students to have said. Surely, one of their statements would be something like, "I now **LIKE** this subject!" Others along this line may come readily to mind. Don't be afraid to dream about affecting their feelings, attitudes, values, and self-concepts, as well as their knowledge and thinking abilities.

_____   _____
    Course Name   Date

Dream List III

KNOW

_____

_____

_____

_____

_____

THINK

_____

_____

_____

_____

_____

_____

FEEL

_____

_____

_____

_____

_____

DO

_____

_____

_____

_____

_____

BECOME

_____

_____

_____

_____

_____

Expand your Dream List further on the next worksheet, making Dream List IV, by imagining what these students would say if you met them five years later, at a reunion or commencement ceremony, for example.

Imagine that one of them comes up to you and says, "Do you remember that course I took with you five years ago? Now that I have graduated and entered the 'real world,' I realize that it was one of the most important courses I ever took because ..." What does this student say to you?

_____   _____
Course Name   Date

Dream List IV

_____

_____

_____

_____

_____

_____

_____

_____

_____

_____

_____

_____

_____

_____

_____

_____

_____

_____

_____

_____

_____

_____

_____

_____

_____

_____

_____

_____

_____

_____

_____

Again, expand the list on the next worksheet, making Dream List V, by thinking about your responses to the students seated before you at the end of the course.

"You know, this was the best course I ever *taught* because ..."

Finish your own sentence.   Then expand it by considering the following variations:

"It was the best course I ever *taught* because:

*   now I KNOW ..."
*   now I THINK ..."
*   now I FEEL ..."
*   now I CAN DO ..."
*   now I AM BECOMING ..."

_____   _____

    Course Name   Date

Dream List V

This was the best course I ever taught because_____

_____

_____

_____

KNOW

_____

_____

_____

_____

_____

THINK

_____

_____

_____

_____

FEEL

_____

_____

_____

_____

_____

DO

_____

_____

_____

_____

_____

BECOME

_____

_____

_____

_____

_____

The more you work on these lists, the richer, more diverse, and better your course will become. Let your colleagues dream with you. Have them help you in expanding your Dream Lists. Reread your course description and content list. See if they give you any further ideas for your Dream Lists.

Carry the Dream Lists around with you for several days. Post copies on your refrigerator, next to your desk, in your car, any place where you will see them. *Continue to add points as you think of them.* Let the ideas on the lists expand and enrich your future course. Some professors have persisted with their Dream Lists over the course of an entire year, jotting down new ideas as they came to them.

Sometimes, college teachers have difficulty with the dream list exercise. Their courses may not seem amenable to this kind of dreaming; disciplinary accreditation requirements may prescribe certain content; they personally find it difficult to carry out. *If one of these, or a similar situation, applies to you, do the following on the next worksheet.*

1. Write a list of substantive topics, content, or subject matter that should go into your course.
2. Describe the topics, content, and subject matter your students *must* have, as distinct from what they could do without.
3. State the goals or objectives of your course.
4. State the skills you expect the students to have when they leave the course.

5.   State the tasks you would like the students to perform in satisfying the requirements of your course.

6.   State the attitudes you would like the students to have during the course and when they have completed it.

7.   What is there in the learning environment that students will need in order to learn in your course?   Equipment, facilities, atmosphere, resources?

8.   What pedagogical issues do you need to consider in teaching your course?   Lecture, discussion, laboratories, computers, homework, exams, quizzes, papers, role plays, debates, etc?

9.   Is there sufficient attention in your course to the contributions and perspectives of minority students and women to motivate them and involve them in your course?

As you write the answers to these questions on the worksheet, include also those points coming to you now for the first time as you think and write.

Course Name   Date

Alternative to the Dream List

_____

_____

_____

_____

_____

_____

_____

_____

_____

_____

_____

_____

_____

B. Analyze Your Dream List

You now have a mostly completed Dream List. It is just mostly completed, since Dream Lists should never really be considered finished. A new idea, which may enrich your course and take it in new directions, may come to you at any time. Keep your list handy so you can write down your ideas as they come to you.

Your mostly completed Dream List now becomes a conscience. It should be a tough master for you. Remember, this is the result of **YOUR** dream for a course. You may change your mind, but at one point you did indicate that the things on this list were ideal. Do not dismiss them or water them down too easily.

It is now time to take your Dream List and develop a course from it, by analyzing it with certain concepts or priorities in mind. Although your Dream List in its totality is important and should be treated as a conscience against which to judge your developing course, clearly some items on it are more important than others; some seem to be more optional than others. Actually there are five categories into which we want you to place the items on your Dream List: Core, Pervasive, and three types of Options — Remediation, Enrichment, and Choice. They are discussed in more detail after a brief definition of the categories.

1) Core

These are the major components of your course. They are absolutely crucial; the integrity of the course would be threatened without them.

2) Pervasive

These are themes, points, issues, or values that are so important they should show up in every unit of the course. The distinction between Pervasive and Core is that a Core item would probably have a specific lesson or week devoted to it, while a Pervasive probably would not. (Although it is possible for a Core item at one point in the semester to become a Pervasive for the remainder of the semester.)

Options

These are also important, but not really Core or Pervasive components of your course. There are three categories of options: **Remediation, Enrichment,** and **Choice.**

3) Remediation

For students who do not have the necessary background for any particular unit of the course.

4) Enrichment

For students who have the background, and also have mastered the content of a particular unit of the course. You exempt these students from the regular assignments and give them Enrichment assignments, perhaps something more challenging, more in-depth, requiring more sophisticated analysis, etc. Alternatively, after students have finished any particular Core, some of them might choose to follow some Enrichment on their own, for extra credit, or to fulfill some further course requirement.

5) Choice

For all students, allowing them to choose among optional items, each related to the same major theme or point. Choices are important, since all students do not have the same strengths, abilities, or interests. Choices allow you to accomplish much more in a course than you ever thought possible. They provide the structure which allows, for example, all students to learn the same basic points, and then follow through on examples of their own choosing.

These categories can be used to analyze your Dream List by providing some structure to the variety of items on it. Therefore, they help you create a real course out of the ideal you created through your dreaming. The way you go about this is to review your Dream List with these concepts in mind.

Core. First look for Core items. These appeared on your list when you initially listed the content in the previous stage. They also probably appeared on your Dream List in response to the phrase, "This was the best class I ever took because now I KNOW ..." On the other hand, if your course is more of a practical one, with clear behavioral objectives, these items may have appeared in response to the prompt, "This was the best class I ever took because now I CAN

DO..."   Regardless of which question prompted the Core items on your Dream List, these will be the basic concepts, learning objectives, units, or topics around which your course will be organized.

Make a separate list of Core items on the next worksheet, or simply designate them as Core on your Dream List.   Many faculty find it convenient to use a different color pen and write a capital "C" next to their Core items. Remember that Core items are **absolutely essential.**   The course could not be called "Finite Mathematics," "Organic Chemistry," "Mass Political Behavior," or whatever, without including these topics.   Be hard on yourself, though, in making this decision. To be sure, everything on your Dream List is important. But some things really are more important than others.   When you get the weight of your discipline, graduate training, graduate professors, or accreditation bodies off your back, what do **YOU** consider the most important topics to be covered in your course?   One mathematics professor we worked with in designing her Calculus course reached a major breakthrough when she realized that she had only three Core content items on her list: the derivative, the integral, and the limit. She realized that everything else was remedial to, an example of, or based on, these three Cores. This realization helped her escape the tyranny of the thousand-page textbook.

Sometimes, faculty look over their Dream List at this point and do not find the kinds of items that would be considered Core at all. In their dreaming, they tend to focus almost   exclusively   on   affective   results,   broad conceptualizations, or terms like "critical thinking," "enjoying,"

Course Name   Date

Analyzing the Dream List
Core Items

---

or "competence." That is fine if you are in this situation. Simply ask yourself more specifically now, "How will I get these affective results?" or "About what should the students be critical thinkers?" or "At what skill will the students be competent?" Answer these questions and place the answers on your Dream List. Once more, we can emphasize that course design is not a linear process. You must go back and forth as you work through it.

Pervasives. As we indicated above, Pervasive items are those themes, points, issues, or values that are so central that they should show up in virtually every unit of the course. Pervasives are very important in making courses our own, but they are the most likely to be lost in the "busyness" of the course. Here is where values, attitudes, and affective objectives often emerge. They likely appeared on your Dream List when you considered what the students might say to you five years later.

For example, perhaps the idea that you want students to love the ballet as an art form showed up on your Dream List for "Ballet I" or "Contemporary Forms of Art." Clearly, Loving Ballet will not appear in your syllabus, nor can it be taught as a Core. You are hoping for a change in attitude among your students. This would be an appropriate Pervasive item. In your dreaming, you felt it was important that students come away from the course with this appreciation. You must now find a way to put it into the course somehow. Since you cannot teach appreciation specifically, it will have to show up in every unit of the course, probably letting your own enthusiasm or love for ballet show itself throughout the course.

Alternatively, sometimes you can teach a Pervasive first as a Core; it then becomes a Pervasive for the remainder of the course. For example, you might teach a method for critical thinking, and then emphasize it throughout the course; similarly for the statistical analysis of data, the matching concept in accounting, or the scientific method in a natural or social science course.

Find the Pervasive items on your Dream List. Label them as "P" or make a separate list for them on the next worksheet. Again, do not be afraid to change your mind on the labeling of certain items. What you thought was a Core may turn out to be a Pervasive, or even a Choice. Be flexible as you work through your Dream List, adding to it, analyzing it, and developing an expanded view of what is possible in your course.

Remediation. Once you have identified the Core and Pervasive items, you need to review your Dream List for Options. As we indicated above, there are several types of Options. Perhaps the easiest ones to consider are the Remediation items.

Review your Dream List for items that fit the Remediation concept, i.e., background material students need in order to master some Core. For many teachers, their lists do not include any Remediation items, since Dream Lists were developed with an ideal conception of the students and the course. Nevertheless, it may be appropriate to consider

Course Name   Date

Analyzing the Dream List
Pervasive Items

_____

_____

_____

_____

_____

_____

_____

_____

_____

_____

_____

_____

_____

_____

Remediation. The most obvious example is in some science courses, where remedial work in math may be appropriate for some students who are deficient. However, it is not unusual with the increased emphasis on writing-to-learn in college courses to find remediation needed for writing. Upper-level courses in all disciplines may also need a remediation unit or two to assure that all students can master the more advanced material. Again, do not be too concerned right now with questions of how you will accomplish the remediation.

Review your Dream List for Remediation items. Consider your Cores with your students in mind. Ask yourself what assumptions are being made that might require Remediation items added to your list. Make a separate Remediation list on the next worksheet or note the items on your expanding Dream List as "R."

Enrichment. Surely, there are some things on your Dream List you have always wanted to be able to teach, but have never really been able to. Look for items on your list that might be considered "advanced" for most of your students, but which nevertheless are more challenging or exciting assignments or topics that you have always wanted to be able to assign to the better prepared students. As one colleague once told me, "I can teach the average students, but I thrive on the better ones!"

Enrichments can replace class time for students who have already mastered some basic concept, and therefore can be released or challenged to do more. We call this approach an Exemption and Enrichment. On the other hand, all students can be assigned to complete an enrichment project, such as in the standard term paper assignment. Enrichments may also be seen as the old "Extra Credit" idea, but when all students have to complete it, rather than just the ones looking for a higher grade. In this way, you can include more interesting, exciting, and enriching topics and assignments into your courses, which have the effect of stimulating the students and enlivening your own teaching. Again, if your present Dream List does not have any Enrichment items on it, consider adding some.

Look for Enrichment items on your Dream List and designate them as such, either on the next worksheet or with a different color "E" on your original Dream List.

Choice. Here is where you provide great flexibility to your course, and some individualization for the students. Students like choices, because they allow a course to be tailored according to their specific goals or interests.

Most often, choices come about in a course when the instructor determines that a basic concept must be learned, but all students do not need to learn that concept through the same specific content. Students can learn the basic concept as a Core item, and can work out examples or applications from among a list of choices. For example, a political scientist teaching International Politics realized that he could teach the basic concepts of a particular core area by allowing students to choose from a set number of options, such as writing a script and producing a videotape, completing a memoir study, synthesizing historical readings, conducting secondary data analysis, or completing a scholarly

_____   _____
    Course Name   Date

Analyzing the Dream List
Remediation Items

_____

_____

_____

_____

_____

_____

_____

_____

_____

_____

_____

_____

_____

_____

_____

_____

_____

_____

_____

_____

_____

_____

_____

_____

_____

_____

_____

_____

_____

_____

_____   _____

Course Name   Date

Analyzing the Dream List
Enrichment Items

_____

_____

_____

_____

_____

_____

_____

_____

_____

_____

_____

_____

_____

_____

_____

_____

_____

_____

_____

_____

_____

_____

_____

_____

_____

_____

_____

_____

_____

_____

_____

literature review. Similarly, an urban sociologist allowed students the choice of studying the literature on the effect of urban crowding on psychological stress, personality changes, or life style changes. Music and art historians have allowed students to choose for more detailed study of a particular period from among a number of composers or artists.

This process is not as dramatically different as it may seem at first. Many college courses require students to write term papers, with the students developing their own topic for the paper. That is simply one variant of the Choice concept. We are suggesting that you might want to broaden that concept to include choices in other areas of the course where they might be appropriate.

In this vein, look over the items you identified as Core and Pervasive. Ask yourself if there are any that are really different examples of the same basic concept. Could students be assigned to choose one or two from among a longer list? *Also look over the items on your Dream List that were not identified as Core or Pervasive.* Are any of them candidates for Choices? Finally, if you do not have any Choice items on your list, *ask yourself if choices might be appropriate at some point in your course.* Add them to your Dream List and indicate them as Choices. As we suggested before, *make a separate list of Choice items on the next worksheet, or use a different color pen to identify them on your Dream List as Choices, perhaps with a "CH."* Do not get inhibited by the concern about how you will specifically organize your classes to accommodate these choices. We will help you with that later; trust us.

Course Name   Date

Analyzing the Dream List
Choice Items

_____

_____

_____

_____

_____

_____

_____

_____

_____

_____

_____

_____

_____

C. Diagram Your Course

Now that you have analyzed your Dream List, placing all items into categories, it is time to begin to order the units into a coherent course. An effective technique for this purpose is to use diagrams as the intermediate step between the analyzed Dream List and the course syllabus. Diagrams transform the ideal found in the Dream List into a structure from which the syllabus can be created. Once this technique is learned, most faculty find that diagramming is more effective than a standard outline, because one can quickly diagram many variations of the same course as new ideas come up. Many professors sit down with a pad of scrap paper, quickly moving from one diagram to the next as they search for one that seems to meet their needs and dreams.

The basic point here is to use boxes or circles to represent parts of your course, connecting them with arrows. You can label as much as you need, since these diagrams are simply for your own purposes. Some college teachers have shown these to their students, however, at the beginning of the course, to give them an overall feel for how the course will be structured. The diagrams seem to communicate better and faster than just a course outline in the normal, written form. It is important to remember, however, that there are no set, hard-and-fast rules here, as in computer flow charts. Use what works for you.

For example, suppose you have four major Core content areas: A, B, C, and D. You could diagram them as in Figure 1 on page 90.

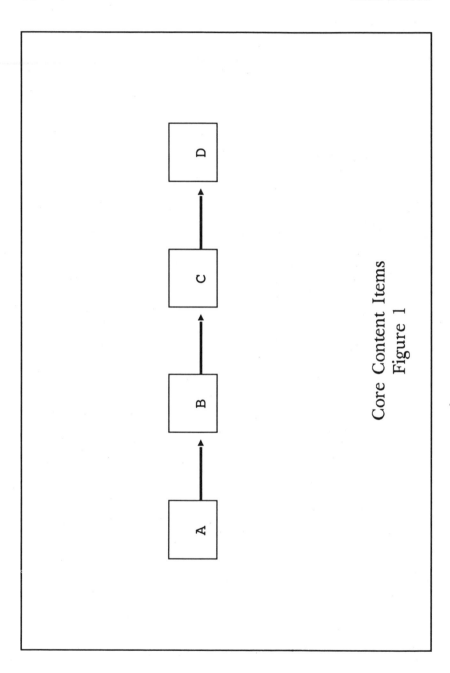

Core Content Items
Figure 1

Suppose, on the other hand, you have three major Core content areas which students must master, but the second one has a variety of applications or examples among which students could choose based on their interests. You could diagram this situation as in Figure 2.

A real example might illustrate the importance and value of providing Choices in your courses, and show how the addition of Choices allows you to accomplish much more than you had ever dreamed possible. Figure 3 demonstrates the situation of an Introduction to American Literature course. Clearly, if all relevant literature is to be covered, this course might require a year rather than the one semester you have for it. The problem, then, is to come up with some way to maximize the coverage of good literature, while still maintaining a one-semester course. The diagram in Figure 3 focuses on a Core area of such a course, Afro-American Literature, and suggests a model for solving this dilemma using Choices. Notice how the use of Choices allows students to read four writers in depth, while being exposed to twenty-two.

Ordinarily, you might begin this Core with an introductory lecture or discussion on the topic of the general place of Afro-American literature in American culture, or an advance organizer focusing on common and divergent themes in this literature. This could be diagrammed similarly to the Core in the B unit in Figure 2. In place of the oral reports, you might arrange for debates or similar in-class exercises designed for synthetic, analytic, and evaluative learning of the whole corpus. A simple box to the right of this diagram would denote the end of this Core, which might be an essay

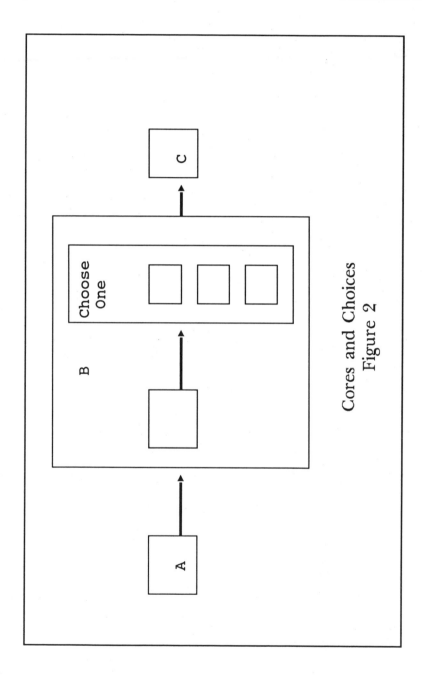

Cores and Choices
Figure 2

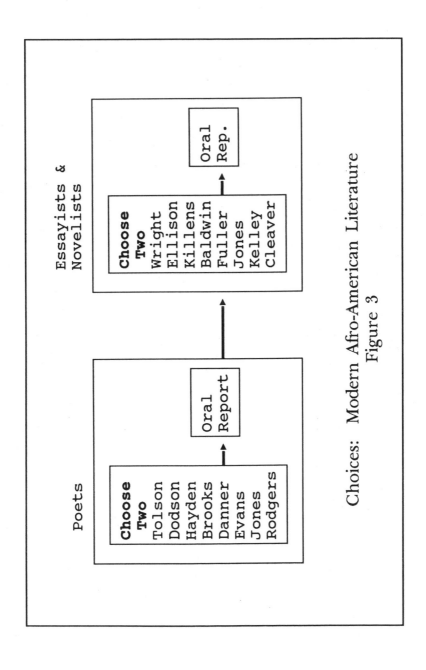

Choices: Modern Afro-American Literature
Figure 3

exam requiring students to know more than the four writers they read, thereby encouraging active listening of the reports or debates.

We encourage you to review *Designing and Improving Courses and Curricula in Higher Education* by Robert Diamond. Chapters 5 and 6, especially, contain numerous case studies and diagrams that further illustrate the use of diagramming for course and curriculum planning. For example, students enrolled in the Introduction to the Study of Religion course (pages 82 and 83 of the Diamond book) are required to choose one unit from each of three lists, but can receive extra credit for choosing more.

In the next example, shown in Figure 4, we demonstrate the introductory module of a course which includes an introductory lecture, a diagnostic pre-test, two Remediation units for students who have demonstrated a deficiency on the pre-test, and the first unit of real content, a Core item. Notice that some students, on the basis of the diagnostic test in history and logic, move right into the first Core, and read Chapter 1. Other students, because of their performance on the diagnostic test, need a history review, a mini-course in logic, or both. Compare our diagram with the one for Economics 201 on page 81 of the Diamond book.

Enrichments could be diagrammed like Remediation in the above example, although for consistency in the diagram they might be better placed above the Core. Suppose, for example, you are teaching a general education course in the social sciences. You have decided that some form of computer-assisted data analysis is a Core component of the course. Some students, however, because of their curricula,

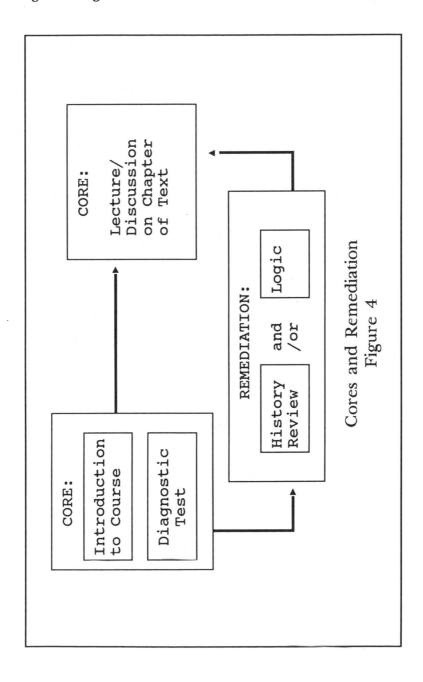

Cores and Remediation
Figure 4

already are proficient at this task. What will you do with them while you teach the rest of the class? If you have them sit through lessons and assignments regarding things they already know, it will bore them and they could become a disruptive force in the class. To excuse them entirely from the two-week period of the course, however, is cheating them and threatens their commitment to the course. Figure 5 suggests one answer to the dilemma.

This example illustrates the provision of an Enrichment for those students who know the material in the Core, as well as Remediation for others who fail to demonstrate competence on either the Core learning or the examination. These students would then get a second chance to demonstrate their learning and/or retake the exam. Notice also we have allowed for the possibility that those students whom we exempted from the core learning might need remediation on their work as well. The awareness that this Remediation possibility might be needed was not initially considered, but emerged from the diagramming process itself. As another example of enrichment, Diamond shows a diagram of a Master's Degree Program in Management which includes an enrichment component on page 92 of his book.

Pervasives can also be included in these diagrams, with their primary purpose being to help us remember to include these ideas or concepts in all components of the course. Suppose you are teaching a general education science course, and wish to emphasize throughout the course the ethics of scientific research. Ethics, then, is a Core item to be introduced and discussed early in the semester, but then becomes a Pervasive as you reinforce the points and indicate

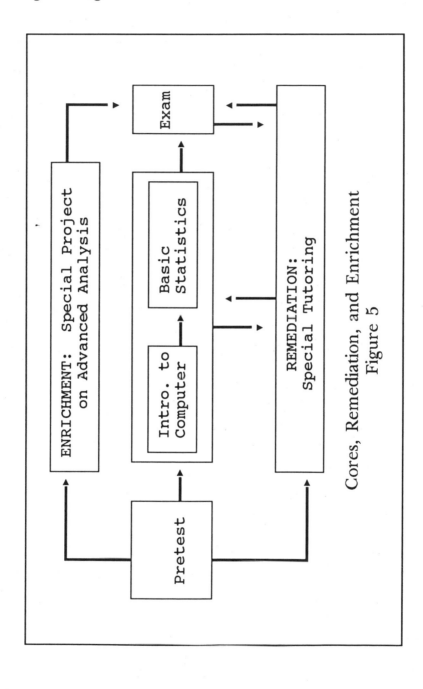

Cores, Remediation, and Enrichment
Figure 5

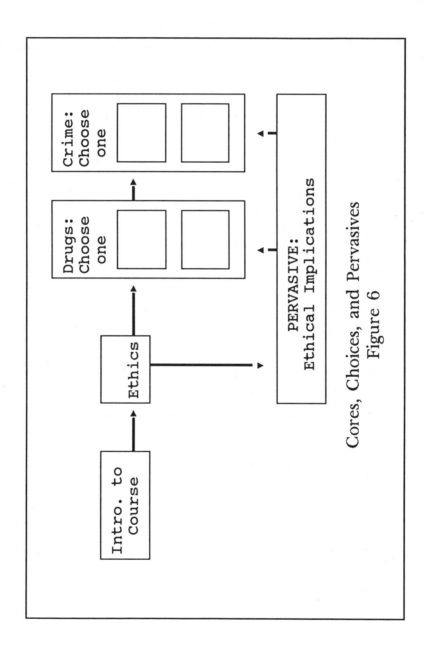

Cores, Choices, and Pervasives
Figure 6

the importance of ethics in all the other Core subjects. The diagram might look like that in Figure 6.

Now it is time for you to try the technique of diagramming on your course. *First, pull out the Core items from your analyzed Dream List, and diagram them on the next worksheet to determine a broadly defined sequence of content. We have provided you with two templates for this exercise, but feel free to use more of your own paper as you experiment with various alternative sequences.*

Diagram of Cores

Diagram of Cores

Now consider Remediation. Do all students have the background to learn each Core, or will some need Remediation before they can proceed? If you expect they do not, are there some Remediation items on your Dream List which could be usefully added here? Try diagramming them following the models shown above. If there are no Remediation items on your Dream List, consider whether you need to place them there. If so, add them and then integrate them into your diagram. If you do not know if the students will have the background, consider a short pre-test at the beginning of each Core. Diagram this pre-test in, following the models shown above. *Look at your Dream List and diagram all the Remediation items into your course on the two-page worksheet. Again, use more sheets of your own paper as you experiment with alternative diagrams.*

Diagram of Cores and Remediations

Diagram of Cores and Remediations

What about Enrichment items on your Dream List? Do they seem to have a natural place in your course diagram? Can they be integrated into the course as Enrichments for certain Cores? Perhaps these could be seen as extra credit options. Maybe you could even require every student to complete a set of Enrichments. *Fit the Enrichments into your course diagram on the next two-page worksheet, but again, do not be constrained by an artificial two-page limit.*

Diagram of Cores, Remediations, and Enrichments

Diagram of Cores, Remediations, and Enrichments

Now consider the Choice items from your Dream List. Are several of them actually different methods of achieving the same objective? Perhaps you could integrate the Choices into the course diagram by providing students with the option of choosing one or two assignments, among several. Are several Choice items actually different topics for students to study, all within a broader, general topic? Is it reasonable to make the general topic a Core, and provide students with Options or Choices of topics within the Core?

Look back to your Course Description, reviewing who the students in your course are and what their probable interests will be. If the course is to be successful for all students, their interests and purposes for taking the course need to be respected. Can you now envision choices for your Dream List you could not imagine before? Do not be afraid to enrich your Dream List from your course diagram. *Work back and forth, developing each one from the other. Answer these kinds of questions while you integrate the Choice items from your Dream List into your course.* Notice that you can include a large number of Choices in your course. When you plan for student reports back to the whole class, the use of Choices results in opening more time in the semester, allowing you to cover more content than you dreamed possible. *Diagram the Choices into your course diagram on the next two-page worksheet, but again, experiment on your own paper with more than just two alternatives.*

Diagram of Cores, Remediations,
Enrichments, and Choices

Diagram of Cores, Remediations, Enrichments, and Choices

Now look at the Pervasives from your analyzed Dream List. If they are truly to be Pervasives, they need to be integrated into every segment of the course. Often Pervasives are values, appreciations, or central ideas. *You need to diagram them in on the next two-page worksheet to make sure you attend to them throughout the course.* Let the Pervasives in your diagram act as an additional conscience, tugging you back to your Dream List, as you continue in the course planning process.

Work through several design possibilities for your course by quickly diagramming them on succeeding sheets of your own paper. Play with various contingencies. Allow your preconceived ideas about what is Enrichment, Choice, Core, Remediation, and Pervasive to change as you work through several different ways to organize your course. Consider sacrificing some content for the addition of skills and attitudes. This is a hard step to take, but it might be worth it.

Look back at your Dream List. Is everything on that list in your diagram? Probably not, but you likely have more in your course than you originally thought possible. Experiment still further with your course to try to get even more in.

Show your diagram to your colleagues. What suggestions are made or occur to you as you explain it? *Incorporate them.*

Diagram of Cores, Remediations,
Enrichments, Choices, and Pervasives

Diagram of Cores, Remediations,
Enrichments, Choices, and Pervasives

D. Work Out the Timing

You are now at the point when you can begin to plan tentatively how much time you will need for each broad section of the course. Pick the first section of the course. How much time will you and the students need to complete it? Move on to the other sections and ask yourself the same question. Then tally up the time to see how close to the semester you have come. If you have more time available to you, great! Look back to your Dream List and course diagram. Consider making some Enrichments into Cores; allow more time for Choices; reconsider Remediations; expand some content areas; provide time for individual or group work on projects.

If you have gone beyond the confines of the time available to you, that is great too! First, consider whether the course you are planning can be expanded into a larger time period. Is it appropriate to teach this course over two semesters, rather than one? Is this question a liberating one? Do you begin to see Options you had not considered before? Great! This is, after all, the course you want to teach! Consider the political and bureaucratic moves required to accomplish this, and get started.

If you cannot justify more time or an additional semester, then take a hard look at your timing. Can you accomplish anything in less time? Take a hard look at your diagram. Are there structural solutions to the problem? That is, is every Core in your diagram really so important? Experiment with diagramming a course without one of them. Could you still defend the course? Can you conceive of a number of related Core items as a group of Choices from which students choose several? Can students complete some of the material on their own, thereby reducing the amount of class time required? Do all students have to do all the work, or can it be divided up with groups of students reporting back to the whole class?

The questions posed above are difficult ones; resist the temptation to find easy answers. Explore these dilemmas and decisions with your colleagues, asking for feedback.

When you have a rough plan for how to fit the course into the time available for it, you are ready for the next phase, **IMPLEMENTATION**. It is not necessary at this time, however, to plan out each specific day or week. That will be accomplished as you complete the next phase.

IMPLEMENTING

♦   Select a Unit and Consider
    the Content

♦   Identify Learning Styles

♦   Write Instructional Objectives

♦   Plan Instructional Activities

♦   Write the Syllabus

IMPLEMENTING

It is now finally time to begin the **IMPLEMENTATION** phase of your course design.   During this phase you will consider all aspects of your earlier work in detail, prepare each "unit" for the classroom, and plan for other details.

How you will actually teach this course becomes a primary concern and influences all the succeeding steps.

A. Select a Unit and Consider the Content

Look back to your course diagram and select a unit or Core area for detailed planning. You are now in a position to be able to plan this particular unit in detail. If your course is sequential, the unit to be worked on should be the first one. Otherwise, pick the one that appears particularly problematic and would benefit most from a systematic approach. Sometimes it is most appropriate to pick the one which has the best or earliest opportunity for testing.

Once the unit to be designed is chosen it is necessary to consider again your students and gather as much information as possible on the learners of this unit. Much of these data were collected and considered earlier, but additional, more specific information needs to be obtained at this point. In particular, it is necessary to consider the skills and knowledge students will bring *to this particular unit.* What assumptions regarding student needs, abilities, interests, and backgrounds are being made? Can you test them out? Are there mathematical or conceptual assumptions for the learning in this unit? Have you considered giving a diagnostic pre-test? If you have taught this unit before, have students had any difficulty with aspects of it in the past? Some faculty members have asked students during a previous semester to imagine what they might like to learn in particular units of a course being planned in a succeeding semester. Do not forget to show this material to your colleagues who are helping you develop the course. Recall also your earlier consideration of Perry's stages of intellectual development. Do you need to reconsider them with regard to this unit?

In recent years, Pat Cross has been advocating the use of what she calls "Classroom Research," the process of involving teachers in the formal study of teaching and learning. She believes that teachers need to conduct research on questions they themselves have formulated in response to problems or issues in their own teaching. Such research, she believes, can act as a powerful motivator for teachers in the instructional development process. In this vein, she has assembled a handbook including thirty assessment techniques which can be used in the classroom by college teachers. These assessment techniques are grouped into three categories: techniques for assessing academic skills and intellectual development, techniques for assessing students' self-awareness as learners and self-assessments of learning skills, and techniques for assessing student reactions to teachers and teaching methods, course materials, activities, and assignments.

Some of the techniques in the second category would be useful as you consider the content of each unit. For example, her "Course-Related Interest and Skills Checklists" are designed to inform teachers of their students' level of interest and skill in course topics. In this technique teachers create checklists of topics covered, and skills strengthened by this unit, or required for succeeding courses or units. Students rate their interest in various topics and assess their current level of skill or knowledge. A similar technique is the "Student Goals Ranking" in which an assessment is made of the degree to which the goals of the students and the teacher's course-specific goals fit or match.   For those interested in more detail on these or other assessment techniques, see *Classroom Assessment Techniques: A Handbook for Faculty* by K. Patricia Cross and Thomas A. Angelo.

On the next worksheet, we have adapted one of the ideas found in the Cross and Angelo book for our purposes here.   *On this worksheet list the content areas of the unit you are planning, specify the skills and knowledge needed by students to learn this material, and state your assumptions about the extent to which you think students have mastered this material when they enter the unit.* This exercise should be repeated for each Core area of the course. It will help you tie the various units together better, assess whether Remediation is appropriate, and plan content in one unit so that students will have it in succeeding ones.

Course Name		Date

Content of the Unit

Content of the Unit	Skills or Knowledge Assumed for This Content	Assumption About Skills or Knowledge
_____	_____	_____
_____	_____	_____
_____	_____	_____
_____	_____	_____
_____	_____	_____
_____	_____	_____
_____	_____	_____
_____	_____	_____
_____	_____	_____
_____	_____	_____

Content of the Unit	Skills or Knowledge Assumed for This Content	Assumption About Skills or Knowledge
——————	——————	——————
——————	——————	——————
——————	——————	——————
——————	——————	——————
——————	——————	——————
——————	——————	——————
——————	——————	——————
——————	——————	——————
——————	——————	——————
——————	——————	——————
——————	——————	——————
——————	——————	——————
——————	——————	——————
——————	——————	——————

Two further, specific areas of instructional design need to be considered here: student learning styles and instructional objectives. Once we have reviewed these ideas you will be able to more adequately plan this unit and the others that follow.

B. Identify Learning Styles

The most useful model on learning styles is that developed by David Kolb. (Much of the following discussion is based on Svinicki and Dixon's "The Kolb Model Modified for Classroom Activities.") Kolb argues that learning involves a cycle of four processes, each of which must be present for complete learning to occur. The cycle begins with Concrete Experience, as the learner receives personal, direct involvement with the material. The next process, known as Reflective Observation, entails the student thinking about or reflecting upon that personal experience from specific viewpoints. On the basis of this reflection, the learner draws logical conclusions or makes generalizations (Abstract Conceptualization), and then tests these generalizations or principles against some form of reality (Active Experimentation). This testing leads to new concrete experience which begins the cycle anew.

Although Kolb believes that all four stages are required for complete learning to occur, he found that students and faculty from various disciplines tend to favor some of these processes over others, or to feel more comfortable in one learning process than another. For example, students in Communications, Political Science, and Sociology favor

Concrete Experience more than those in Physics, Chemistry, and Engineering, who feel more comfortable with Abstract Conceptualization. Similarly, people in Educational Administration and Accounting are more comfortable with Active Experimentation than those in Philosophy or English, who tend to favor Reflective Observation.

It is unnecessary for you to administer the tests Kolb uses to determine the learning styles of your students. The implications of Kolb's ideas for course design are that different instructional activities may support different phases of the learning cycle, so that, in the ideal, courses should be designed so students are led through the full cycle for each major content area. For example, students in a history class might first be exposed to films or written reports about historical events. They could then be asked to write reflective, personal reactions to that experience, which would be followed by a lecture and discussion on the period. The cycle would be completed with an assignment asking the students to apply principles learned about this period in the earlier phases of the learning cycle to a different historical era. The Svinicki and Dixon article includes several such examples from different disciplines for the reader feeling uncertain about how to apply these principles to the course being designed.

A view of learning style differences that is different from Kolb's is found in the research using the Myers-Briggs Type Indicator (MBTI). The MBTI also identifies different preferences for learning and researchers have identified teaching and course design implications of these types. For those who are interested in this view of learning styles see

Campbell and Davis, 1990, for a brief review and further references.

At this point, integrate these considerations of learning styles into your conceptions and assumptions about the students, and this unit in particular, on the next worksheet. Do you have any new ideas about this unit based on these considerations? Make any changes that now seem appropriate and repeat this exercise for every Core unit.

_____   _____
      Course Name   Date

The Learning Cycle
for This Unit

Concrete Experience

_____

_____

_____

_____

_____

Reflective Observation

_____

_____

_____

_____

_____

Abstract Conceptualization

_____

_____

_____

_____

_____

Active Experimentation

_____

_____

_____

_____

_____

C. Write Instructional Objectives

Much of the literature in course design stresses the importance of preparing instructional objectives as a course is being designed and taught. Surprisingly, however, there is little research demonstrating that students learn more or better when instructors develop instructional objectives. Some research suggests, though, that teachers benefit from the preparation of such objectives, because the process focuses their attention and helps them to organize their teaching.

Most literature on instructional objectives takes a behavioral approach, which considers the outcomes of learning in observable and measurable terms, including a precise criterion of success. Some examples of such behavioral objectives include:

"After completing this unit, you will be able to write in a half hour, a simple computer program that calculates the mean of a set of data points."

"After completing the instructional activities in this unit, you will be able to pass a one-hour multiple choice exam, with 85% of your answers correct."

"After completing this unit, you will be able to critically evaluate *The Color Purple* by Alice Walker based on your knowledge of the learned helplessness of battered women."

An especially useful, and brief, source for those who wish more information on objective writing is *Preparing Instructional Objectives* by Robert Mager. Do not assume, however, that all learning objectives must be stated in this format. Many instructors in the Humanities, for example, find it difficult to state precisely behavioral outcomes for their literature courses, or to objectify affective goals in this fashion. Still, attention paid to stating, or at least considering, goals and objectives is a very beneficial planning activity, because it helps focus our teaching. Simply asking, "Why am I assigning this project or reading?" or "What do I hope the students will get out of this unit?" will go a long way toward focusing our courses, assignments, and use of class time.

The consideration of learning objectives is also important because they have a direct bearing on the teaching strategies you choose. A useful model to aid you in this activity is Bloom's taxonomy of educational objectives. (Much of the following discussion is taken from "Teaching Techniques for Instructional Goals: A Partial Review of the Literature" by Larry Lovell-Troy.)

In Bloom's taxonomy, educational objectives are ordered hierarchically; learning at higher levels depends on the attainment of skills and abilities at the lower levels. The basic elements of this taxonomy are knowledge, comprehension, application, analysis, synthesis, and evaluation. Objectives at the **knowledge** level ask students to state information from memory, but these goals imply more than a random recollection of facts or definitions. Ideally, a student should be able to organize the facts into a context or scheme so that they make some sense. Therefore, the teaching and learning process must provide information to the student within such a context or scheme. Lectures, using handouts, asking rhetorical questions in class before lecturing to students, and stopping a lecture after fifteen or twenty minutes to have students share notes or ask each other questions before asking them in class are all good teaching strategies for objectives at the knowledge level.

When your objectives are at the **comprehension** level, your expectations are greater. Now your goal is to have the students be able to paraphrase, to understand the material, and to restate it in their own words, to interpret information, or to extrapolate trends. Therefore, the teaching and learning process must be more student-centered for comprehension because students need time to attempt the task, receive feedback, and try again. A small group discussion organized around the interpretation of significant passages in a text is a good teaching strategy for objectives at the comprehension level, as are small group discussions requiring students to work together on other questions for which there is no one correct answer.

At the **application** level, the student is asked to apply concepts and understanding from one context to another or to engage in some problem-solving activity. Typically, you would teach students a method for engaging in this activity and a set of rules about how and when this method should be applied. Case studies, asking students to bring relevant newspaper articles to class, and student journals, diaries, and autobiographies are all good strategies for teaching and learning objectives at this level.

Objectives at the **analysis** level ask the student to break down a thesis or idea, such that its component parts are clarified. Included here are such goals as recognizing unstated assumptions, checking the logical consistency of an argument, and recognizing the organizational form or pattern in a work. The instructor needs to be sure that students already have mastered the content at the comprehension level, as well as a model or set of principles for how to analyze. Teaching strategies at this level include diagramming on the board the argument in a work, and then asking students to do the same for a different work, debates, in-class writing assignments, and small group discussions revolving around critical thinking and analysis of texts or arguments.

At the **synthesis** level, objectives are similar to what is regarded commonly as creativity. The goal is for the students to put together parts or elements in a new way to create an original pattern or structure. Students often have a difficult time with this objective, primarily because they tend to reify it. At various levels of their education they have seen fellow students who seem to be quite intelligent and creative, but few teachers spend time teaching students *how* they can be creative. Consequently, creativity seems to be an inborn quality rather than the result of hard work. Thus the awe with which students view "creative" people prevents them from realizing their own potential for creativity. The teaching and learning process, therefore, must include classroom support for discussion, diversity of backgrounds, personal growth, divergent thinking, and openness. The message must be very clear that students are never ridiculed for making slightly off-the-wall contributions to classroom discussions. Furthermore, students need to see through example that creativity comes from hard work at the comprehension, application, and analysis levels. Brainstorming in class with follow-up analysis and assignments to write stories, diaries, poems, or the like which draw on *both* an analysis of textual material and personal experiences are two examples of teaching strategies for this level of objectives.

Evaluation is the highest category of the taxonomy and requires the incorporation of all other levels. Students at this level are asked to make a judgment and to state their rationale or criteria for that judgment. These criteria may come from an internal analysis of the situation, in which case evaluation is an extension of analysis, or they may come from some external criteria such as standard theories or known works, in which case evaluation is an extension of synthesis. Most students will need to be taught models for how to do this, however, because it assumes that they are at Perry's stage of relativism, and research suggests that few students attain this stage during college. Consequently, the best teaching strategy for this level is to work in class on methods of how to evaluate and provide support, feedback, and practice.

Based on these considerations about instructional objectives and teaching strategies, use the next worksheet to develop learning objectives for this first unit and begin to consider how these objectives can be met. Again, it is not necessary to state all the objectives in the formal language found in the literature of instructional design. If that style suits you and your course, fine.   Otherwise, it is simply important to specify what you want the students to learn at each point in the course, the learning level in Bloom's taxonomy, and what the appropriate teaching strategies for these objectives would be.

_____   _____

Course Name   Date

Learning Objectives and Teaching Strategies

Learning Objective	Bloom's Level	Learning Strategies

Learning Objective	Bloom's Level	Learning Strategies
_____	_____	_____
_____	_____	_____
_____	_____	_____
_____	_____	_____
_____	_____	_____
_____	_____	_____
_____	_____	_____
_____	_____	_____
_____	_____	_____
_____	_____	_____
_____	_____	_____
_____	_____	_____
_____	_____	_____
_____	_____	_____

D. Plan Instructional Activities

Notice that the course design and teaching implications of Bloom's taxonomy of instructional objectives dovetail with Kolb's ideas regarding learning styles, as well as with Perry's concepts of students' intellectual levels. The actual teaching of a course requires careful consideration of all these models.

Review the learning resources list you completed in the **GATHERING** *stage. On the next worksheet fit the appropriate sources into the unit plan as developed on the past few worksheets. Plan the instructional activities for this unit so the students gain experience in as many learning processes as possible.* Do not hesitate, however, to expand that list now that you have the particular unit in front of you. Are there commercially available materials that would fit your objectives? Are there people with whom the students could consult as part of their learning? Films, demonstrations, field trips? Do you need to prepare your own learning materials for the students?

All activities of the learning sequence should be planned and prepared at this time, including:

* lectures
* discussion formats
* other teaching techniques
* instructional materials not prepared earlier
* diagnostic tests
* student manuals or guidelines
* commercially-prepared texts and/or materials

* space and facilities, including transportation, if needed
* grading procedures and instruments
* evaluation techniques

Once you have completed this process for the first unit you chose to implement, move on to the next unit. Follow the process for the remaining units of the course, in turn. Many of the materials you purchase or prepare can be pre-tested; others cannot. Pre-test anything possible. Show these materials to your colleagues. Show them to trusted students who may be similar to those who will be in the class. Sometimes it may be possible to integrate them into a different course on a trial basis to see how they work. Take the feedback from these pre-tests seriously. This step can lead to a successful unit or one that just muddles through.

_____   _____
        Course Name   Date

Integrating Your Learning Resources
into Your Unit Plan

| | Learning | Learning |
| Content | Strategies | Resources |

_____   _____   _____

_____   _____   _____

_____   _____   _____

_____   _____   _____

_____   _____   _____

_____   _____   _____

_____   _____   _____

_____   _____   _____

_____   _____   _____

_____   _____   _____

Content	Learning Strategies	Learning Resources

E. Write the Syllabus

Once you have diagrammed and/or designed all the units for the course, it is time to write the syllabus. This should be more, however, than a daily or weekly outline of the course. It is really a contract with the students; you will help them learn certain material in exchange for their commitment and attention. Accordingly, the syllabus should state what you expect of them and how you will teach the course.

Specifically, the syllabus should contain at least eight basic types of information. (Much of this section is based on "Syllabus Shares 'What the Teacher Wants'" by Howard Altman.) First, personal information about you and the course serves as a sort of preface. List the course name and number, meeting time and place, and your name and phone and office numbers. Second, include a basic course description. You might use the course description written during the **GATHERING** phase of the course design process, and revised along the way. You might also want to describe your teaching philosophy to the students at this point. Two courses with the same course description taught by professors with different teaching philosophies will be quite different in their actualization. The course objectives are the third component of the syllabus, and can be pulled from those written above for each unit. Again, students' learning can be enhanced if they know what is expected of them. At this point you might also want to consider including the course diagram you developed as you planned the course. If it helped you to conceptualize the course as a whole, it might help the students to gain a similar appreciation.

Fourth, write, in as much detail as possible, the course calendar with relevant dates, assignments, and exams. Students appreciate detail and clarity here to help them understand the ebb and flow of the work for the course. Remember, yours is not the only course students are taking. Fifth, a course requirements section should specify what the students are expected to do in the course and how they will be evaluated. If attendance, class participation, quizzes, and homework will be evaluated, they should be specified here. Sixth, state the materials and experiences from which students will learn. At a minimum, describe the readings; at a maximum, include all sources from your learning resources list here or in the calendar section earlier. Seventh, indicate the procedures used to evaluate students' learning with the percentage weights for each method.

Finally, a statement that the course syllabus is subject to change offers a protection for you and for the flexibility of the learning process. Syllabi are legal documents, and both professors and students can be held to them. Nevertheless, flexibility is important in a college classroom, because each class is unique. Teaching these particular students may require different amounts of time, instruction, or evaluation than you had planned. The best path to follow, therefore, is to plan as much as you can, but always be open to changing your plan. The course is designed for the students' learning, not to "cover" the material.

Based on these considerations, write your course syllabus on your own paper.

```
┌─────────────────────────────────────────────┐
│                                               │
│   TEACHING AND EVALUATING                     │
│                                               │
│      ◆    Plan Teaching Strategies            │
│                                               │
│      ◆    Evaluate Your Course                │
│                                               │
│      ◆    Revise Your Course                  │
│                                               │
│                                               │
└─────────────────────────────────────────────┘
```

TEACHING AND EVALUATING

A. Plan Teaching Strategies

It is finally time to teach the course you have designed. However, teaching involves more than just lecturing to the students. It is a complex process that involves many decisions along the way. A well-designed course may not be taught well because of poorly conceptualized pedagogy. On the other hand, it is also true that "good teachers" can often carry a poorly-designed course through their skills of clarity, organization, and reaching students.

As you follow through on your planned teaching strategies and begin to teach your course, there is one cardinal rule that must be kept in mind. *Students must be motivated through interaction with you and the material; the material by itself will rarely motivate most students.* Motivation comes from involving the students in their learning, and they must be motivated and involved all along the way. Otherwise, they will not feel ownership of their learning, or of the course, and classrooms may become battle scenes with the students pitted against the faculty member. Active learning is the key.

There are many other lists of principles for effective teaching in the literature on college teaching, but few are better than those proposed by Arthur Chickering and Zelda Gamson. Their list of seven principles includes active learning or involvement, respect for the diversity of the students, high expectations, opportunities for feedback, student-faculty contact, time for students to practice what is learned, and cooperative learning. (See their "Seven Principles for Good Practice in Undergraduate Education" for further details on these principles.) Review the articles by Svinicki and Dixon and by Lovell-Troy for many other suggestions along these lines. *Remember, always ask yourself as you plan each class period, "Is this the most involving way this material can be learned?"*

Do not forget your colleagues at this point either. They can offer good advice. *Ask them to come into your class, take notes, and meet with you afterwards. Consider having yourself videotaped and review the tape with them.* Always keep yourself open to improvement in teaching, as you will also keep yourself open to improvement in the design of your courses.

B. Evaluate Your Course

It is crucial to evaluate each unit of your course, as well as the total. There are basically two sources of data for this evaluation: measures of student learning and measures of student feedback. *Both are important, and you should routinely obtain both when you teach.*

The most important form of evaluation is the measure of how much the students have learned, since that is the reason for the course. The most easily accessible sources for this evaluation are the examinations, term papers, performances, or other forms by which you test your students. Their performance on a fairly developed test is your best form of feedback. It is important to keep in mind, however, that tests are not just measuring student learning. They are also an evaluation of your teaching. If students do well, you have succeeded.

If students do not perform well, it is necessary to consider the reasons, and develop solutions. There are at least three important questions to ask yourself. First, are the students studying properly? If not, what can you do to change their study habits for this unit? Second, was the test a fair measure of their learning? Often tests are inadvertently designed to measure learning not taught during the unit. Look back to your objectives for the unit. Does

the examination test the satisfaction of these objectives? If
not, is there a better way to measure the students' learning?

Sometimes   we   teach   at   the   Knowledge   or
Comprehension   level,   but   test   at   the   Application   or
Evaluation level. To expect students to Apply or Evaluate
their learning on an exam when we have not given them an
opportunity to practice these skills under our tutelage may
not be the best approach. If you find that students are not
performing well on your exams, this may be the problem.
If so, consider your objectives. If your goals are at the
Knowledge or Comprehension level, test the students at that
level.   If you want the students to be able to Apply,
Synthesize, or Evaluate, be certain that you spend time in
class reviewing these skills as they apply to your course
material.

Finally, does the unit need revision? Perhaps the
problem is with the teaching or planning of the unit. Review
your course design with special attention to where the
problem might be. Were the students ready for this material,
or did they need remedial attention? Was the unit pitched
at too low a level, which had the effect of boring the
students, resulting in inattention? Are the objectives of the
unit reasonable for these students at this school at this time?
Did the instructional design fit the objectives and prepare the
students for the measure of their learning?

The important point to keep in mind here is that the
performance of students on any test is more than an
evaluation of student learning. It is also a measure of the
test itself, the course design, the appropriateness of objectives,
and the strategies used to teach the material. In cases where

students do not perform well, it is necessary to consider all options.

Formative evaluation is the term given to student feedback oriented toward course improvement, an additional and important source of data. Contrary to disgruntled faculty scuttlebutt, most students want to learn, and are decent evaluators of how material is presented to them. Often, they may even have good suggestions for improvement.

Numerous objective ratings are available and are easy to administer. Most of these have the specific kinds of questions needed to evaluate teaching and course design. Such instruments are also easy to develop on your own. Questionnaires with objective ratings are appropriate to administer at the end of a particular unit, perhaps along with the examination which evaluates students' learning. If you are particularly interested in a specific assignment, on the other hand, attach a set of questions to the assignment, asking students to hand it in anonymously.

Less objective evaluations can be obtained in a class discussion or brief written assignment, and these are often more useful than objective ratings. Simply ask the students to answer questions such as: "What has been going well for you in this course? What has not been going well? Do you have any suggestions for improvement?" Students can be grouped to discuss their answers to these questions, and group reports turned in to you to preserve anonymity.

In our discussion of considering the learners of the specific units, we introduced Cross's ideas about "Classroom Research." Some of her techniques for assessing student reactions to teachers are certainly appropriate for this section of the course design process because they can assist professors in the collection of student perceptions of their courses. Cross suggests such techniques as electronic mail messages, chain notes, one-minute papers, and quality circles.

The type of evaluation used, whether objective or narrative, is less important an issue than is the necessity for frequent evaluation. This is especially important when you are teaching a re-designed course for the first time. All evaluations should be saved and consulted for the next step.

C. Revise Your Course

No matter how well you have planned and followed the guidelines offered in this workbook, a course is never really completely designed until you have finished teaching it for the last time. You change each time you teach it; new groups of students enroll in your classes; the field changes; the teaching materials change; the curricula in your department and college change. All of these changes require you to teach a slightly different course, perhaps each time you teach it. Chapter 10 in the Diamond book, referred to earlier, describes four case studies of course revision following evaluation.

Revision of your courses is therefore a constant part of being a teacher. Using the suggestions in this workbook, including the constant attention to evaluation, makes the process easier, because you will be better able to focus on the particular aspects of your course needing attention. Although a completely new design for a course may only be necessary a few times, constant revision of units or sequencing may be required each time you teach it. The process, however, keeps you growing and improving as a scholar and a teacher, and ensures that your courses will continue to improve.

Good luck!

Glossary

Abstract Conceptualization. The stage in Kolb's experiential learning cycle in which the learner draws logical conclusions from observations.

Active Experimentation. The stage in Kolb's experiential learning cycle in which conclusions and generalizations are used to guide decisions and actions.

Active Learning. A style or philosophy of teaching and learning in which the learner is engaged personally in a cognitive or emotional way with the content.

Analysis. An objective in Bloom's Taxonomy of Educational Objectives in which the learner is asked to break down an idea into its elements or parts.

Application. An objective in Bloom's Taxonomy of Educational Objectives in which the learner is asked to employ concepts or understandings from one context to another.

Choice. One of the options used to analyze a dream list in which students are allowed to choose among several learning units, each of which satisfies a similar educational goal or objective.

Comprehension. An objective in Bloom's Taxonomy of Educational Objectives in which the learner is asked to understand, interpret, or extrapolate information.

Concrete Experience. The stage in Kolb's experiential learning cycle in which the learner becomes personally involved in a specific experience.

Content List. A list of all possible content that could be included in a particular course.

Core. A major component of a course, which is absolutely crucial to that course. The integrity of the course would be threatened without its inclusion.

Course Description. A step in the course design process in which an attempt is made to describe the course as completely and from as many perspectives as possible.

Course Design. The process of creating a plan by which students will learn a body of knowledge.

Diagram. A schematic model of the course, used to help uncover alternate arrangements of content and material, and to communicate in a picture the essential outlines of the course.

Dream List. A list of ideal images for a course. It is developed in the course design process in an attempt to expand the course content and teaching techniques beyond those traditionally included in courses in any particular field, and to uncover affective, pervasive, and central goals of a course.

Dualism. The earliest stages in Perry's intellectual development model in which knowledge is seen as a collection of facts to be memorized and teachers are authority figures with all the answers.

Enrichment. One of the options used in analyzing a dream list in which students can be offered a more in-depth or sophisticated option when they have mastered the content of a particular unit of learning.

Evaluation. Feedback in the designing, learning, or teaching process. The evaluation may be formative or summative. It may be of the students, the teacher, or the course, or all three at once. Also, an objective in Bloom's Taxonomy of Educational Objectives in which learners are asked to make judgments and critiques, and state their criteria for such judgments.

Exemption and Enrichment. A particular type of enrichment in a course design when a proficient student is exempted from regular course work and given an enrichment assignment.

Faculty Development. The process of assisting faculty members with the improvement of their teaching, courses, or career.

Formative Evaluation. Evaluation oriented toward course or teaching improvement.

Gathering. The step in the course design process of collecting as much information about the course as possible, including a course description, a description of the learners, a content list, and a learning resources list.

Implementing. The step in the course design process in which the details of the course are elaborated. It includes planning each unit more specifically, reconsidering the learners of those units, identifying their learning styles, preparing instructional objectives, planning learning activities, and writing the syllabus.

Instructional Development. That part of faculty development specifically oriented toward teaching and course design.

Instructional Objectives. Statements about what the learners should learn in any unit of a course.

Knowledge. An objective in Bloom's Taxonomy of Educational Objectives in which students are asked to learn information within a context or scheme.

Learning Resources. The sources from which teachers and students learn. The materials teachers use to focus their students' learning.

Learning Styles. Personality characteristics or orientations toward learning that vary among groups of students.

Multiplicity. The middle stages of Perry's intellectual development model in which uncertainty is acknowledged in some areas, but when facts are not known all opinions are seen as equally valid.

Options. Categories used in analyzing a dream list which allow for great flexibility in a course design. Three options exist including remediation, enrichment, and choice.

Pervasive. A category used in analyzing a dream list in which basic themes, values, or issues of a course are identified. Pervasive items should be included in virtually every unit of a course.

Planning. The step in the course design process in which the information collected in the gathering stage is expanded and organized. It includes creating a dream list, analyzing the dream list, diagramming the course, and working out the timing of each unit.

Reflective Observation. The stage in Kolb's experiential learning cycle in which the learner thinks about a new experience from many viewpoints, seeking to find its meaning.

Relativism. The later stages of Perry's intellectual development model in which students can understand and appreciate that facts are often a function of context, and decisions need to be based on supporting criteria. Authorities are seen as simply more experienced learners.

Remediation. One of the options used in analyzing a dream list in which students without the necessary background for any particular unit are given an opportunity to learn it.

Summative Evaluation. Evaluation oriented to global measures of a course. These are often used in personnel decisions.

Syllabus. The contract you establish with the students which specifies a course description, expectations, course content, schedules, forms of evaluation, and the like.

Synthesis. An objective in Bloom's Taxonomy of Educational Objectives in which the learner is expected to put together elements in a new way to create an original pattern or structure.

Taxonomy of Educational Objectives. The classification of learning objectives developed by Benjamin Bloom and his colleagues in an attempt to clarify learning objectives and the creation of examinations. It includes Knowledge, Comprehension, Application, Analysis, Synthesis, and Evaluation.

Bibliography

Altman, H. 1989. "Syllabus Shares 'What the Teacher Wants.'"
The Teaching Professor 3:5 (May).

Banathy, B.H. 1991. *Systems Design of Education: A Journey to Create the Future.* Englewood Cliffs, NJ: Educational Technology Publications.

Belenky, M.F., Clinchy, B.M., Goldberger, N.R., & Tarule, J.M. 1986. *Women's Ways of Knowing: The Development of Self, Voice, and Mind.* New York: Basic Books.

Bloom, B.S., Engelhart, M.D., Furst, E.J., Hill, W.H., & Krathwohl, D.R. 1956. *Taxonomy of Educational Objectives: The Classification of Educational Goals. Handbook I: Cognitive Domain.* New York: Longman.

Campbell, D.E. & Davis, C.L. 1990. "Improving Learning by Combining Critical Thinking Skills with Psychological Type." *Journal on Excellence in College Teaching* 1:39-51.

Chickering, A.W. & Gamson, Z. 1987. "Seven Principles for Good Practice in Undergraduate Education." *AAHE Bulletin* (March).

Clinchy, B.M. 1990. "Issues of Gender in Teaching and Learning." *Journal on Excellence in College Teaching* 1:52-67.

Cross, P.K. & Angelo, T.A. 1988. *Classroom Assessment Techniques: A Handbook for Faculty.* Ann Arbor, MI: National Center for Research to Improve Postsecondary Teaching and Learning.

Diamond, R.M. 1989. *Designing and Improving Courses and Curricula in Higher Education.* San Francisco: Jossey-Bass.

Eickmann, P.E. & Lee, R.T. 1976. *Applying an Instructional Development Process to Music Education.* Syracuse, NY: Center for Instructional Development.

Frederick, P.J. 1981. "The Dreaded Discussion: Ten Ways to Start." *Improving College and University Teaching* 29:109-114.

Frederick, P.J. 1986. "The Lively Lecture — 8 Variations." *College Teaching* 34:43-50.

Fuhrmann, B.S. & Grasha, A.F. 1983. *A Practical Handbook for College Teachers.* Boston: Little, Brown.

Gilligan, C. 1982. *In a Different Voice: Psychological Theory and Women's Development.* Cambridge, MA: Harvard University Press.

Goldsmid, C.A. & Wilson, E.K. 1980. *Passing On Sociology: The Teaching of a Discipline.* Belmont, CA: Wadsworth.

Grasha, T. 1990. "Using Traditional Versus Naturalistic Approaches to Assessing Learning Styles in College Teaching." *Journal on Excellence in College Teaching* 1:23-38.

Kolb, D.A. 1981. "Learning Styles and Disciplinary Differences." In *The Modern American College*, edited by A.W. Chickering and Associates. San Francisco: Jossey-Bass.

Kolb, D.A. 1984. *Experiential Learning: Experience as the Source of Learning and Development.* Englewood Cliffs: Prentice-Hall.

Lovell-Troy, L.A. 1989. "Teaching Techniques for Instructional Goals: A Partial Review of the Literature." *Teaching Sociology* 17:28-37.

Lowman, J. 1990. "Promoting Motivation and Learning." *College Teaching* 38:136-139.

Mager, R.F. 1975. *Preparing Instructional Objectives.* Belmont, CA: Fearon.

McKeachie, W.J. 1986. *Teaching Tips: A Guidebook for the Beginning College Teacher.* (8th ed.) Lexington, MA: Heath.

Perry, W.G., Jr. 1970. *Forms of Intellectual and Ethical Development in the College Years: A Scheme.* New York: Holt, Rinehart & Winston.

Stark, J.S. & Lowther, M.A. 1986. *Designing the Learning Plan: A Review of Research and Theory Related to College Curricula.* Ann Arbor, MI: National Center for Research to Improve Postsecondary Teaching and Learning.

Svinicki, M.D. & Dixon, N.M. 1987. "The Kolb Model Modified for Classroom Activities." *College Teaching* 35:141-146.

Taub, D.E. 1991. "Strengthening the Social Within Social
     Psychology: An Experiential Learning Approach."
     Teaching Sociology 19:186-192.

Index

ABOUT THE AUTHORS

Larry Lovell-Troy is an Associate Professor of Sociology at Millikin University. He has been a full-time college teacher for over fifteen years, having previously taught at Indiana University at Fort Wayne.

As Millikin University's first Consultant on Teaching and Learning (1984–1987), Lovell-Troy conducted numerous workshops for his colleagues on teaching and course design. He also provided individual counseling with teaching, course design, and student evaluation issues to a large percentage of the Millikin faculty.

Lovell-Troy has been a staff member of the Great Lakes Colleges Association Workshop on Course Design and Teaching since 1986, providing individual and group assistance on teaching and course design to over 150 faculty members. He has given workshops and presentations on teaching and course design throughout the Midwest, and has served as a consultant to colleges establishing faculty development programs. He is the author of two articles on college teaching and other publications in the sociological fields of race and ethnic relations and family.

He lives with his wife Mary, a social worker, and their two children and three cats in Decatur, Illinois.

Paul Eickmann has held various appointments as a music faculty member for approximately thirty years. Most recently, he held a dual appointment in music and education at Syracuse University. During that time, he also held several major administrative positions. For eight years, he worked full-time with faculty members at the University in course and curriculum development. During that time, he was the Associate Director of Development at the Syracuse University Center for Instructional Development.

Eickmann was a staff member of the Great Lakes College Association summer workshop entitled "Course Design and Teaching." He worked individually with over 250 faculty members from a wide range of predominantly liberal arts colleges during his thirteen years with that workshop.

He is the author of numerous articles on the topic of course and curriculum design and has given workshops and presentations at more than 50 colleges and universities in this country and in several foreign countries.

Presently, he is Vice President for Academic Affairs at the Cleveland Institute of Art.